SACRAMENTS

SACRAMENTS

HUGH LAVERY

Darton, Longman & Todd
London

First published in 1982
Darton, Longman & Todd Ltd
89 Lillie Road
London SW6 1UD

© 1982 Hugh Lavery

ISBN 0 232 51504 2

British Library Cataloguing in Publication Data

Lavery, Hugh
    Sacraments.
    1. Sacraments
    I. Title
    234'.16   BV800

    ISBN 0–232–51504–2

Phototypeset by Input Typesetting Ltd, London SW19 8DR
Printed in Great Britain by The Anchor Press Ltd
and bound by Wm. Brendon & Son Ltd
both of Tiptree, Essex

CONTENTS

1

HOW PEOPLE COMMUNICATE

The joy of all living and all loving resides in the ability to communicate. Man is a voice: he must speak, or die of despair and isolation. The hardest punishment man can inflict on man is solitary confinement. He can endure many privations, hunger, cold, torture and brutality. What he finds unendurable is total isolation. This destroys him. It is not good for man to be alone; it is evil. It is death.

Yet in some sense every man and woman is alone and must be alone. For every man and woman is unique, singular in taste and temperament. I am I, he is he, she is she. Mankind knows no replicas, no duplicates. There is likeness; there is never sameness. Yet man and woman share much in common. That common inheritance we call human nature, and this is the clay from which all are composed. Each of us here is born and each will die. Birth and death bracket all human existence. Each one is driven by desires; desire for life, liberty, and the pursuit of happiness. Each of us wants to succeed, even to excel, to find that completeness named fulfilment. Each of us wants to be recognized, to be accepted. Therefore, each of us needs some other. To be recognized, to be accepted, demands someone else; someone who accepts me as I am without conditions. I cannot survive in a desert, cannot live without company, cannot bear total silence and solitude. So, living is living with. I cannot become myself without some other person. Uniqueness does not mean isolation, for isolation inhibits growth, but relation nourishes it. And the best bonding is shared experience. This is the magnetism which creates small and large communities, families, clubs, tribes, nations, state and Church. Those groupings are not accidental; not optional but necessary. They answer the great demand, that strains and stretches every heart, the demand for the other.

Yet, man and woman do not share everything in common. Human nature does not exhaust man's composition or disclose all

1

his capacity. Indeed, the most engaging, the most eloquent, the most magnetic quality in any man or woman is an element he shares with no other man or woman. This fine spark that burns brightly and differently in each nature we call personality. Nature is the clay of which all mankind is compounded. Personality is different. Personality is the singular force, the spirit which draws and attracts and makes for differentiation. It is difference that brings delight; it is monotony that repels. The highest compliment paid to anyone can be condensed into three words: 'You are different'. Or even: 'You stand alone'. There is a healthy aloneness. Each man and woman is, and must be alone, if they are to be themselves. They must not abdicate singularity. This aloneness is the obverse of their uniqueness, the very salt of personality.

Men and women are born endowed with human nature. The child in the cot is fully human in its needs for food, warmth and affection. It cries, it smiles, it wakes and sleeps. It loves the light and fears the dark. It wants company and caress, and its first word is 'Mother'.

The child is a parable of all human nature, humankind in miniature. But the child is not a parable of human personality. Human nature is given; a universal legacy, the common denominator of all mankind. Personality is promise, and is experienced as possibility; it is the chancy element in everyone. It may grow and find realization, find greatness, even glory. Or it may remain sterile as a stone. Nature and personality are not interchangeable. As the child is endowed with human nature, we can easily identify with its condition which speaks through weakness and dependence. The child is charged with possibility and may become an outsize personality. Nature in the child is complete; personality is germinal. It is a seed; a seed seeking good soil, seeking the sunlight, and this potency we denote by the word 'promise'. The child, we say, is full of promise. Promise is the present reaching for the future, for no one can live without some future. Every child, even the deprived, has promise and there is no more engaging word in the language than promise. For promise is bright with the future, and its horizon is wide, its scope infinite. It looks to the stars. The glory of the child shines in its promise, for promise suggests hope and renovation. This child may become what I have failed to become, a real and rounded personality. It is always in the child

2

that we see hope of fulfilment and hint of greatness. For this child is unique, instinct with the promise of greatness and glory.

The secret of Christmas, its beauty, its attraction, is the birth of a child of promise. Even an agnostic and uncertain world will not let go of Christmas. It still incarnates the unspoken hope of all men, for hope stirs and breathes in the birth of a child who promises to renew this battered place and to be a light to all who live in darkness and desperation.

The child, then, is human in its nature but promising in its personality. It is wiser to describe it as a human becoming than as a being. Yet, a question mark hangs suspended over the head of every child. Will the child's becoming end in being, in being somebody, and terminate in greatness? Or will the child's becoming end in nothing, in being a nobody, end in futility and frustration? Will the child realize its personality? Or will it remain ungrown, its personality stunted, its talent unused, its life without increase, its death unmourned and unmemorable? Will the spark break into flame, generating heat and light that will renew the face of this resisting earth? Or will it flicker and fall, and be quenched like a useless candle? Will its life be an April of wonder or a winter of waste? This question hangs over every child. And the answer depends. Depends on other people. Not on luck or accident, not on money or charm, but on connections made or refused. This is the choice.

Choosing is the act which decides every human destiny. To be – or not to be. That is the question. Personality is not self-realizing, not effortless increase. The first five years of the child's life are years of dependence and may be decisive for the next fifty. The first influence is the mother. She communicates her own reading of reality to the child. The world of the child is the world of the mother. Mother and world are almost coterminous. Maternal communication is the first communication; communication of life itself.

It is communication largely without speech, for speech is not the only or even the most eloquent agent of communication. The most eloquent communication is touch. The infant which is warmed and well-nourished but never stroked will sicken and die. The child needs touch more than talk, needs to feel the love in the hand pressed on a head, the comfort of a caress, the cover of an embrace.

3

This need is universal and does not die. The other person is never superflous. Hence, the adjective most evocative of true communication is the adjective 'touching'. I found that play touching. It was a very touching experience. Touch is the first sign of affection. 'Don't touch me' is the great negation, the sign of disaffection, chosen refusal.

The vocabulary of communication is the vocabulary of sign, not merely for religious people but for all mankind. Signs convey interior attitudes. The mother's regard for the child can be mediated only through signs, caring and consoling signs. Love is an abstraction. It does not come to us like rain. It is always mediated, and the agent of mediation is the sign.

What we call reality is all maze and mystery and needs an interpreter. It is too intricate for understanding: the best mind cannot explain it. The world presses too heavily on everyone and there are opposing interpretations of its origin and purpose. But the question cannot be evaded. And the key question concerning reality is one. 'Is reality friendly or hostile?' Those poems and plays, films and novels which we call classic ponder this question. Is good or evil the stronger force? Is life merely to be endured or can it be enjoyed? Is the world a lost place with no good and no God and with no one to guide? Is there nothing to live for, to hope for, to die for? These questions make the heart-murmur of the human race. Men cannot answer by analysis, for the hinterland of reality cannot be seen by straight vision. The reality you see and I see is filtered through finite things we call signs. No one has ever seen pure light; only a lamp or a star, or a grey dawn. Pure, unoccluded light is denied to man. Man wants to see directly. He sees through smoked glass, and the light is dim, bent and refracted.

Light is experienced both as sign and as reality. All people employ this language. When Christ says, 'I am the light of the world', he uses sign-language. But what men see is Jesus, a man. When Christ says 'You are the light of the world', that too is sign-language. But what men see is a community. The vernacular of communication is sign, and common speech is largely the dialect of sign. Thus, we read in the newspaper of an actress that 'She became a star overnight'. We understand what is meant. Or, in the summer of 1914, when Edward Grey looked out of his window one evening and saw the lamplighter, he remarked to his wife,

'The lamps of Europe are going out one by one'. We know what he means. Light is used as a sign. You may say of a woman, 'Her smile is like the morning'. It makes sense. Light, lamp, star, dawn; these are signs that make the best alphabet available to man. They alone make communication possible, and we cannot dispense with this coinage.

For the helpless infant there is only one sign that gives access to reality: the mother. It is the mother who gives the first tentative answer to the unavoidable question, 'Is reality friendly or hostile?' The mother answers only by signs, touch, song, frown, smile, gesture; these communicate her life and her love, her joy or her despondency.

The pre-natal life of the child is one of total protection. It is life without demand. Possibly a lingering nostalgia for the life of the womb stays with us all. Everyone seeks a protector and the womb is the matrix of total protection. But the child is created to be a personality and must be born. Birth is the first trauma every-one undergoes. When born, the child cries; a cry of pain. For this is the first experience of separation.

People fear separation, separation from the safe, the cosy, and the undemanding. That is always painful; painful as dying. The new-born child has died to the life of connection, of safeness. Once the umbilical cord is cut the child is, in a real sense, alone and exposed. This is his first dying and it cries at the pain of parting, at the sorrow of being born. Yet dying is the price of being born, both in infancy and in adult years. It is a price we do not want to pay. Yet the growth of personality demands a series of dyings and risings. This is the cadence of the human condition, decline, fall, rise, renovation. This is the rhythm of the seasons, autumn, winter, spring, summer. This is the sequence of the day, night, dawn, noon, evening.

Reality is read through signs, and this reading must never end. It is in this sense that Christ admonishes us to be children, to remain pupils eager to learn and to live with a child's faith in the future, in the future as open and with promise of glory. Promise sustains the child. For the child is totally unlike the animal. The animal is endowed with quick powers of survival which we call instincts. The lapwing chick, which seeks to break out of the egg, will receive a signal from the mother if danger threatens. The unborn chick will remain totally still. Already it can read and pond to a danger signal. The chick ceases to move and refuses to emerge. Though not yet born, the lapwing is already provided with an instinct to sense danger and to assure survival.

The child has no such instinct. Everything has to be learnt. The child is the creature that is totally vulnerable. It is not partially dependent, but absolutely. It cannot feed itself; someone must feed the child. The child's need, then, is not just biological, not just an animal need. The child's need is personal. It needs the mother, not just for food but for affection. The need is total. The mother-child relationship is the ground of personal existence. Other relationships presuppose this first foundation.

It is from this experience that we may find what 'personal' means. 'Personal' derives from the relation of persons, by communication with some other, The new-born child demands a relationship which is not animal but personal. The infant, then, lives by communication; it can live no other way. Communication is the meat and drink of personality, and growth in personality is through the expanding ability to communicate. The babe in arms is already communicating by the most potent sign of human affection, by touch. This is communication and this already is communion, half-realized, wholly enjoyed.

The classic picture of the Madonna and Child is the most engaging symbol of what being a person means. For the heart of personality is reciprocity, stimulus and response, give and take, I and thou. The Madonna and Child is a sign, a touching picture, a moving experience. Our Lady's function as mother is not incidental or decorative. The infant in the crib depended totally on Mary for food and affection. The infant grew in wisdom and stature through communication first with Mary and Joseph. The child grew in holiness, not in isolation but in the closeness of the Holy Family. The Holy Family was not superfluous to Jesus; it was necessity. The Church is not additional to sanctity. It is essential. In the home at Nazareth Jesus learned. Learned what? That reality is friendly, not hostile, that it is good to be here, that life has point and purpose, that its fuel is love. From Mary who was sinless and full of grace he learnt that the force which governs and guides reality is an unconditioned love.

This is a lesson worth learning and sad people never assimilate it, for there is a competing emotion seeking to possess every heart. This emotion is fear and it can become the presiding power. Its claims are many and its claims are persuasive. So much depends on those early years and on the emotion which pervades the home. The child who knows that it is loved, no matter how fractious, will perceive the world as good and will respond by giving love and affirming life. Indeed the child who knows it is loved makes all the gestures and signs of one who feels it is good to be here, and privileged to be born. But it does not know this by instinct for it is not an animal, not an instinctual creature. It learns this only by signs, and the primary signs are personal. Only a confident person can relay them. Love itself is a blur. We cannot see love, cannot define it. It is real but invisible. Love is mediated, as life is mediated, by signs charged with unusual voltage.

The child wakes in the night, sees nothing but darkness and it screams. Screams what? 'Mother.' Mother runs upstairs and switches on the light and says 'There's nothing to be afraid of, I'm here'. This is communication by effective sign. Not merely word but action and presence and person. This is communication of the love which exorcizes fear, fear of the night, fear of the unknown. But this action of the mother's is an assertion of a truth and of a faith. She switches on the light. This is an assertion that there is light in the world, which is stronger than darkness and that this light is always available. She says, 'There's nothing to be afraid of'. But is this the truth? Is there always a someone, symbolized by the mother, who will save the child from the unknown and from the night? Is there a light in the world or will the sun grow cold and darkness enclose the world?

The need of the child is a personal need, need for the real presence of the person who protects. This need of the child, because personal, endures in the adult and endures till the end. The great need is for a saviour. Every adult is always under assault from the night and the unknown. Fear is the cause of isolation. We need the other; yet we fear him and fear her. So we refuse to communicate. This fear is deep and tenacious. Yet this fear can be dispelled. No one can release himself or herself from this hell. Someone must speak, someone must come, someone must relay light and love. And liberation. We need a sign that there is a Someone who will respond to that cry of the heart. And, as the need is for a person, than that sign must be a person.

Christ is that sign sent to reveal that God is father and mother and love unlimited, master of the night, lord of the unknown. So

7

it is not mere metaphor when he proclaims himself, 'Light of the world'. Without light we cannot live, and the only sufficient light is not knowledge. The sufficient light is the person, but a person who withholds nothing and gives recklessly. So the life of Christ cannot be understood unless it is seen for what it is. The life of Christ is totally giving and forgiving. Only this person can save and satisfy. The life is communication at white heat. The great revelation of Christianity is that in God there is endless interchange, complete reciprocity, action and reaction, communication without inhibition. Father and Son totally diverse yet completely one through the Spirit that animates and unifies. This is revelation not merely of God but of the hidden heart of reality.

It is at this point that we glimpse, however dimly, the genius of personality, which is the genius of free and glad communication. And here we glimpse, however dimly, a little of the meaning of that elusive word 'love'. The need for love is universal. It is the only ache of the heart. Christ reveals that human love does not meet human aspiration. All human love is limited, transitory, conditioned and fragile. The loved one so often does not meet expectations.

The predicament of man may be that he seeks from another man or woman a love they cannot impart. The good news is the answer to the question 'What is love?' The answer, 'God is love', reveals something precious. It reveals first of all that the heart of reality is friendly, benevolent, on our side. But men persist and naturally ask, 'If God is love, what kind of love?', and the life of Christ gives answer to the question of what is love in a world of warfare.

Christ is the sign we seek. He is the voice and his alphabet is the alphabet of sign. It is not natural, not easy, not common to see reality as kind, and God as concerned. This must be learnt; this must be communicated. And communication takes two; one who speaks and one who hears. Christ is the revelation that God is not cold, impassive and impersonal. Christ reveals that in God there is total communication, total diversity and total unity. We can see this in part and experience it in part because we are made in that image and in no other.

This revelation speaks to our desire. Each one of us is called to be unique. This seems to suggest detachment as the recipe for self-realization. Christ reveals this as a false reading. We realize

8

personality not through reserve but through relationship. This requires long, life-long schooling. Indeed relationship is not easily understood. It begins with regard for the other person's unique-ness, in acceptance of the other person's difference. But it consists also in regard for my own uniqueness and for my own difference. These two must be held in tension; regard for the other's unique-ness and concern for my own.

This makes relationship possible, but relationship is always a tension, a marriage of dependence and independence. Every relationship involves surrender but not self-annihilation. Every relationship involves give and take, invitation and response. But authentic relationship does not fence freedom; it enlarges it. Authentic relationship is grounded on parity, and it cannot survive with domination and submission, with master and slave. An adult mature relationship is grounded on parity. Love cannot live with compulsion, with demand or with servility. The phrase, 'You must love God', or 'You must love me', is meaningless. 'Must' and 'love' do not go together. Love is a free offering completed by free reply.

Christ reveals the quality and character of love. The lover is the one who lets me be myself and helps me to become more myself. Relationship, when genuine, reveals that difference does not mean incompatibility. Father, Son and Spirit are wholly different and wholly compatible. God is the totally personal. Christ reveals that personality is both our ache and our aspiration. Each one of us wants to be unique and that is good. But we cannot realize our uniqueness on an island, only in relation. The question occurs, 'Is this rare and refined relationship possible to man, or must it remain just an echo?'. The answer is that to man it is not possible. But with God all things are possible. But how can man be with God? Only by response to God's invitation. His offer is not a word, but a word made flesh and blood, a divine person, a man human. This is God's sign, fully personal, and this sign is the secret of sacrament. But sacrament takes two, one who gives and one who receives. The act of receiving we call faith. And faith is free response.

So God works not through pressure but through persuasion, not through threat but through attraction. Love is the attracting force. Sacrament cannot be understood unless we see every person as in some way sacramental. We are using sign-language, sacra-

9

mental language every day. If I say, 'He is a hard man', I am employing the vocabulary of sign. How do I know he is hard, how do I know she is warm, how do I know God is good? How do I know God loves me as I am now? Only by signs. Signs make the grammar of sacrament.

The final question, 'How do I know whether this big, untidy universe is friendly or hostile?' The answer is simply, I do not know and cannot know. There is so much pain, evil, crime, so much darkness, so much death. I need a sign that the light is stronger than the dark and that love is stronger than death. Mere teaching, mere talk are not sufficient. We are persons and we need personal signs. Above all, we need a person who has undergone every human experience, who has been born, rejected, buried. And yet has transcended all the death forces in the world, come through them, risen from death and hell and is vividly alive. Alive in a people. That is the sign we seek and that is the key to sacrament.

We cannot understand sacraments if we see them as things, as rites, as ceremonies. Sacrament is not just a word and action. It is personal. Only the personal will satisfy. That singular sign, that personal sign is Christ. We cannot survive unless we know that, present in this dark world, there is a Light, that there is a Someone riding above the malice and meanness in the world. That Someone we name in a fine word, 'blessed'. Christ is the blessed one; he is the blessed sign. He is the Saviour and he is the Blessed Sacrament.

2

THE LANGUAGE OF SIGN AND SYMBOL

One of the most memorable and moving paragraphs ever inscribed in English was written by the Dean of St Paul's in his room as he heard the great bell tolling for a funeral. The question occurred to him, 'Who is being buried this afternoon?' A natural question. Then suddenly it seemed to him a foolish question. And he took his pen and wrote a paragraph that the world still intones after many centuries.

> No man is an island, entire of itself. Any man's death diminishes me because I am involved in mankind. And therefore never send to know for whom the bell tolls. It tolls for thee.

It is a passage both pensive and melancholy, easily remembered. It speaks tenderly and its tone is Christian. Because it sees mankind not as an aggregate of isolated entities. It sees mankind as a body, and it has one revealing phrase: 'Any man's death diminishes me because I am involved in mankind'. This simple sentence is biblical in mood, a paraphrase of the noblest Christian teaching. St Paul would be proud to have written it, for Paul invokes the metaphor of the body and sees mankind, and indeed the whole of creation, troubled by the labour of gestation, always seeking to be born, to be unified, to be one in aim and endeavour.

The body is a visual symbol of difference, variety finding cohesion. There is no more potent image of diversity-in-unity than the body. The body is so various: head, heart and hands; nerve, muscle and bone; yet all animated by one impulse, a model of co-ordination. The body remains the indispensable image to all who speak of the unity of mankind. The state is the body politic; the Church the body spiritual. What everyone seeks is the body of mankind, working in unforced collaboration.

This is man's oldest dream. But does the dream remain a dream? Can it be realized? Does the body of mankind exist only as an ideal? Or can it truly be embodied? Common sense says

'No'. Common sense sees every man as an island, self-seeking, self-enclosed, often lost, often alone. Hell, says one philosopher, is other people. I think we know what he means. Getting away from it all is a universal desire. Isolation, though cold, often seems preferable and we all experience the desire for forgotten islands, for quiet and unpeopled places.

This, then, is the human dilemma; man is alone yet needs other people. From experience we learn that man cannot live a solitary life. He must go out, speak and hope for reply. But where are the agents of connection? How can one isolated individual speak to another? The agents of connection we call signs and symbols; this makes the language of sacrament. Signs and symbols are not interchangeable, not synonymous and not to be confused.

A distinction between sign and symbol is necessary for an understanding of sacrament.

We are all familiar with signs. People who drive cars respect signs. The Highway Code is the guide book of the good driver. He is expected to read the signs. But the sign is conventional and man-made. The school sign used to be a torch; now two children holding hands. For the sign has no built-in connection with the thing signified. Connection is accidental. The sign is simple; one to one. Red means danger. But the sign is arbitrary. We use blue for Our Lady, but blue tells us nothing about Our Lady. White could be substituted. Why then do we have signs? Signs are for simplification. They are facilities; they make life easier. Traffic signs simplify driving. Every map is sign-language. Kitchen equipment has its signs; also medicines and mathematics. But sign does not explore; does not probe, does not illuminate the deep and dark places of existence. Signs tidy experience, give it shape, make it orderly and manageable. In this country we have adopted metrication. Why? Because it is easier than imperial measurement.

Signs then, are facilities though they can have emotional overtones. A song, a street name may recall an event. But men and women cannot live by signs, just as they cannot live by algebra. Signs are reality as surface; they operate only in the world of object, in the world of things. A surface-world does not satisfy. Why? Because we all need and seek to journey within, to reach below the rim of consciousness, to explore and explain experience. We want more than the real, we want the Really Real. Here the sign is insufficient. It orders; it does not illuminate. And it is illumination all men seek, for we live in a dark and dangerous universe.

For the Christians, the primary sign is the sign of the cross; it identifies the Christian. A cross in someone's lapel denotes a Christian. A cross on the cover of a book signifies a religious and Christian book. A cross on a map marks the location of a Church. Yet the cross is more. It is not an exclusively Christian sign. It is universal, what psychologists call 'archetypal'. Long before Calvary, Christ says, 'Take up your cross daily'. People understood him.

The cross means the daily diet of adversity, the pains and perplexities which test us all. Every people, every culture, every civilization employs the cross to signify the weight and worry of experience. For the Romans, the cross was a sign of degradation. The lowest class in the Roman empire was the slave-class and capital punishment for the slave was crucifixion. In life, the slave was a symbol of debasement. In death he reached total degradation. And the Jews themselves saw crucifixion as the great curse; 'There is a curse on the man who hangs on a gibbet'. The death of Christ was not only torment but degradation. Christ in his life offended the pious and respectable by mixing with outcasts, with the diseased, with the failures and the fallen, with that breed of people good Jews named as sinners. They avoided outcasts to resist contamination. Christ sought their company. He loved sinners. This was the scandal that attended his life and made certain his death. On a cross.

In his death he was degraded and the cross was the sign of his regard for the rejected. He was rejected by the pious, rejected by Peter, and numbered with the world's great losers. The first Christians were appalled when the cross became their badge of identity, for it argued a servile status and spoke of their subjection. The cross became acceptable only when the image of the risen Christ was impaled there. Here the cross, a sign of victimization, became a sign of victory. Here the cross as a sign of disgrace became an emblem of grace. The cross, a sign of death, became a sign of life-through-death. The present crucifix is a thirteenth-century innovation. It presents Christ as dead or in torment. The original crucifix presented Christ risen and alive, beyond pain,

13

beyond hell, beyond death. The badge of death was made the symbol of glory.

The cross which, to the secular world, remains a sign, now for the Christians becomes a symbol. It is not inert but active. It does something. It recalls an event. It conveys two meanings; the meaning of death and the meaning of life. And so it revises the accepted meaning of death and hell and life as impasse. And it reveals that love is not sentiment but sacrifice; that love is not soft but strong. It is sacrifice which gives love its steel and its stamina.

Christians venerate a cross now become a crucifix. It is more than a sign now, more than a badge on a lapel; it moves and it remembers. It defines a new attitude to reality. It is responsibility accepted; it is faith affirmed. Its meaning is not pain and its mood no longer pathos. The crucifix was veiled in Holy Week because it was a symbol of joy and victory. The unveiling of the cross on Good Friday was greeted with acclamation; victory evokes applause. Possibly here we can begin to glimpse something of the difference between a sign and a symbol. It is not easy to grasp. Briefly, a sign points to the thing signified. A symbol re-presents the thing signified. 'Represent' means to make present.

Signs are created by man. The arrow with the word 'diversion' informs the motorist he must turn left. It is a sign made by traffic commissioners. It is man-made and will be removed; its function is simply to point. Symbols are deeper. Symbols precede man; they are born out of life and they convey life. You may ask, What are they? And where are they? The answer is, simply, everywhere. Read the first page of the Bible, the first page of Genesis, and you enter the world of symbol. There is no man or woman, no animal or angel. Yet there, on that page, is the great blaze of God mediated through the genius of symbol. The first sentence begins with what? With nothing, with void. How can anyone present 'nothing'? Only by symbol. That primeval sludge and slack water convey waste and nothingness, a fearful picture that appals by its lack of form, colour, beauty. That is symbolized deadness; an anti-world with no light, no leaf, no life.

This is nothingness pictured in language a child can understand. The child's word for nothingness is 'rubbish'. 'You are rubbish.' This is the language of symbol. And this is the universal vernacular of man. And of God. Man's great fear is annihilation, the onset of nothingness. Man's great desire is life. And all life comes from

14

God. In the Genesis picture God's spirit impregnates the grey slime and brings deadness to life. And this life is mediated through tangible and visible and attractive things; through light, water, sun, sky, field and flower.

These are all creations of God, and all arteries of life. These are not mere signs; they do not merely point. They present. They do not merely inform; they transform. Symbol has vigour and voltage. Without water, oil, bread and wine, men cannot live. So we talk of the water of life; of bread as the staff of life. Yet water is not enouth and bread is not enough. They are necessary but insufficient. Man needs the Spirit if he is to be what he aches to be. This is the stir of our restlessness. And this is what prompts ambition. No man can disown the image in which he is made, and the divine impress cannot be erased. Man seeks God by impulse. He calls it the search for life, the search for meaning, the search for security. But most movingly, the search for love. We seek God under many names.

The work of Christ is to read reality for us, to disclose that the language of creation is a chorus to the Creator. Christ sees the finger of the Father pressed on creation, and feels the breath of the Spirit singing or sighing in every creature. He sees water as a reality in its own right, but not self-enclosed and not self-explanatory. We see water as a symbol of a higher and invisible reality. To make this clearer he prefixes an adjective to water to emphasize its symbolism. The adjective is 'living'. 'Living water' is that which conveys the spirit of God, the life of God.

Christ is seeking to convey the true reading of reality; it is symbolic and sacramental. This is a new language and needs to be learnt. People are not naturally endowed with this literacy. The western world does not easily understand symbols. Our secular society is sacramentally illiterate and sees reality largely as surface, seldom as symbol. This impoverishes all understanding. The farmer sees a field and can assess its fertility. The botanist sees a flower, can classify it, and detail its characteristics. But this is a limited approach to reality. The schoolboy is asked, 'What is water?' He answers, 'H_2O'. A thin answer and a symptom of the western approach to reality. It understands things by their components. So the great question such as 'What is man?' becomes unanswerable. The schoolboy has been taught to see water as thing, as matter, as self-enclosed, as just the sum of its components. Reality is presented as unsymbolic, as insignificant; it does not lead to any other reality, does not convey any other reality. Reality is pointless. And so life disappoints.

All of us here have inherited this threadbare reading of reality and it has made the world weightless and religion outmoded. The real has been equated with the thing. The real (we suppose) is the tangible, the machine, the gadget. Is that all there is to reality? If it is, man's predicament is, indeed, hopeless. Is a flower just a thing and nothing more? What of its beauty? Is beauty illusion? Or is it a revelation? Christ looks at the flower and its beauty speaks of the beneficence of the Father. Christ sees water as liquid, but also as symbol of a higher reality which mediates what man needs to quench a stronger thirst. We are moving now into the world of sacrament and of symbol. It is not the received western understanding of reality. Sacramental vision really demands new eyes, eyes that see through the surface to the symbol. You can see with the eyes or you can see through the eyes. What we see with the eyes is the finite, the thing, and the world is a supermarket. But the Really Real, the great realities, cannot be seen or priced or bought. 'Can't buy me love', as the song says, But western eyes see narrowly. The good is goods, the world a warehouse.

Television is endlessly preaching a theology of the market. 'If you get this thing, you get confidence.' This has now reached a point of puzzlement. Many people are wondering if the thing is all there is. Because if that is all, then life becomes a matter of accumulation. People now ask if affluence brings beatitude, if possessions create happiness, if the good life consists in goods in over-supply.

This is Christ's great either/or. Either God or money. Both are good; only one is God. The temptation to settle for the thing is man's first temptation; it begins with the eyes. We see reality as things. And the packaging is attractive. The shop window is so seductive that we think 'Here is all I need'. Christ says we need more; we need the sublime. But how does man reach the infinite, the eternal, the sublime?

The avenue to the infinite is through the finite. There is no other access. The Really Real is mediated to us through symbols. There is one error fatal to the understanding of sacrament. It is this: to think there is reality plus symbol. No so. Reality is in

16

symbol and not independent of or antecedent to it. There is no direct road to the Father. Christ says, 'No one can come to the Father except through me.' This simple sentence is worth pondering. This simple sentence deepens the Christ-approach to reality and to religion. 'No one can come to the Father except through me.' What is the revealing word in that sentence? The revealing word is the preposition 'through'. 'Through' is indispensable to those who seek to penetrate the crust of creation and go within.

Symbol is misunderstood by those who say 'It's only a symbol.' This reveals a misunderstanding of the genius of symbol and of sacrament. Symbol is not reality-diminished. It is reality-enlarged. Symbol is not reality-minus; it is reality-plus. We can go to the Really Real only through the finite. We cannot dispense with this preposition 'through' even in prayer. We must end each prayer, 'through Christ our Lord'; this is the Christian condition. The preposition is the key and it secures the value and validity of symbol. This is the grammar of reality Christ is trying to expound, which the liturgy is seeking to evoke, and which the poet is seeking to illumine. When the poet writes, 'The world is charged with the grandeur of God', this is the eye alert to symbol. It is not the mundane reading of reality. Many would deny this assertion; they do not see the many-splendoured thing. Many see with the eyes; few through the eyes. 'The world is charged with the grandeur of God', is a fine sentence. It goes through the finite to the infinite, through the surface to the centre; through the secular to the sacred.

All this is necessary to the understanding of sacrament. The psalmist writes, 'The heavens declare the glory of God.' Do they? This is the language of symbol; not of sight, but of insight. The western world and western education have largely lost this sacramental perception; poetry, art and religion all stand on the defensive and this is the cause. The disease of the western world is an eye-disease, an astigmatism which has narrowed vision so that men see only things as surface. But they are not satisified. The great question is, 'What is the Good?' And the answer given is that the good is the thing which can be used. The last secular symbol is the status-symbol. It is a symbol of affluence. The long limousine declares not what I am, but how much money I have. This is decline; this is corruption. Once men and women are assessed by what they have, then they too have become just objects. For so often, the more you have, the less you are.

The consequence of this surface understanding is superficiality, and an interior emptiness. If the thing is the only reality, then how can you live? Only by acquisition. Such a laborious existence. Life is no longer being but having. Love is no longer giving but possessing. The person can no longer be loved, only be used. 'We must cultivate his friendship; he may be useful.' The principle of conduct becomes utility and then despair finds its voice. It complains that life is meaningless and that God is dead. In a sense he is, for those who see through envious eyes. Men cannot live on utility. The best things in life are not earned but given. It is hard to accept that what we earn is less valuable to us than what we are given. Family, friends, life and love, these are given things, gracious things. Given to those open to their reception; seen only by those with eyes who can see 'heaven in a wild flower'. That is sacramental. That satisfies.

Children have imaginative eyes and find wonder in a world full of glory. For children live on the given. Their world is grounded on grace not on utility, on what they receive, not on what they earn. The young child easily believes in Santa Claus, because he sees the world as gift. The adult, however, must face the roughness of reality and acquire the discipline of work. The counter-temptation is to see nothing as given, nothing as grace, and to accept as the leading text, 'In this life you get what you pay for'. Here begins the idolatry of work. This is life deprived, life as hard labour. This is not the truth. What we deserve and earn and acquire by effort are of far less moment than what we are given. The ability to work, to teach, to make and manufacture are given things. Without health and ability we could do nothing.

Our disease is reduced awareness, false consciousness, a failure to see things as they are. Christ comes to enlarge awareness, to rectify consciousness, to make us see reality through clear and unacquisitive eyes. Christ is totally aware that everything he has, he has received from the Father. His dominant emotion is gratitude. 'Father, I thank thee.' He seeks to impart to us that same releasing emotion and to liberate us from living enviously. We say in the Mass, 'Father, we come to you with praise and thanksgiving.' Praise! We praise only the praiseworthy. Praise is appraisal; appreciation of the good. Thanksgiving is the noblest

emotion and the most liberating. It is acknowledgement that we live on grace not on merit. My heart is beating at this moment not through my own volition, but through a divine impulse.

Christ is the first sacrament. Not merely a sign of grace, a pointer, but an agent of grace; a creative symbol. What we call sacraments are ordained occasions when we communicate with Christ and meet his invitation with free reply. So in each sacrament we take an active part. The sacrament of marriage, 'Will you take this man to be your lawful wedded husband?' 'I will.' In the Mass, 'The body of Christ. Amen.' Baptism, 'Are you willing to be baptized?' 'I am willing.' This is dialogue; this is sacrament. We cannot appreciate sacraments unless we see the whole world as sacramental and creation as carrying the signature of the creator.

But we need visual aids and there are many of those blest with receiving eyes. There is creation itself; there is the liturgy of the seasons. And there is the sacred liturgy of the Church. But above all, there is the person. And no matter how disfigured or defaced, the image of God is somewhere present in each afflicted person.

Mankind is always asking for peace and always oppressed by war and contention. It is hard to see one's self as totally involved in the travail and trials of mankind. But to see the self as involved is to put on Christ. Christ did not lament the world; he loved it. The world is so lovable that he died for it. He asks me to see myself as called to save and serve the body of mankind. This asks for new vision and kind eyes; sacramental eyes. After all, what is the Church? Merely people, that community of people whose values are in tune with Christ's, who relay Christ's generous attitudes. The Church itself can never be understood unless as a symbol, as a sign that this world is good and is God's world. This symbol conveys his joy to a world tempted to see death as final and life as futile.

The Church must identify with the world when confronted with the death-things because these impose their weight on every consciousness. Death is the temptation to disbelief. Yet the Church celebrates a death. But in the Church, death is seen not as disaster, but as the agent of life and a glimpse of glory. But we need sacramental eyes. With Christ death becomes charged with meaning, becomes sacramental. Death is seen as a fertile extinction and Christ, speaking to country people, borrows a rural metaphor.

19

Death is a seed put into the soil which must die if it is to bring forth corn and bread for man's invigoration. All this is revelation. And revelation is always hard to receive. The Church is commissioned to impart it. But we cannot impart what we do not, in some sense, understand.

Christ sees the world as in travail. 'Something is afoot in the universe', one writer says. 'Something that speaks of birth and gestation.' This is mankind's universal urge to become one. And this is both attractive and a cause of despair. So many people feel alone and isolated, they see creation as cold and man as vile, beyond rescue and redemption. That is not the vision of Christ; that is not the vision of the Church. The Church is called to relay life and love to people uncertain of both. Many good people see themselves as alone and unwanted, forgotten by God, rejected by man. But the truth is otherwise. We are all part of one great continent. 'No man is an island entire of itself.' Any man's death diminishes me because I am involved in mankind. And, therefore, never 'send to know for whom the bell tolls. It tolls for thee.' This is the ring of truth.

3

THE BORN AND THE BAPTIZED

With baptism we enter into the world of sacrament and that world is not the next world. It is this world. Sacraments belong here and this restless world seeks one sign: that life is not meaningless. It looks for a sign to show that life has point. It looks for a person who knows both the way and the end. This person must be involved in the mess of things, and undergo the pain of our experience. He must be vulnerable to hurt, be lifted by joy, acquainted with sorrow. He must, some day, die. He must not only be in the world, but in a real sense, over the world. Because if the world could disarm him, malice would have dominion, evil would wear the crown. We would walk a doomed and dismal place, on the margin of desperation.

Christ, the sign, is a man like other man, born of woman and with no protective armour from daily assaults. Yet, he speaks with a new accent, with a felt authority. He lives and he dies, yet unlike other men. He is a man not partly possessed by the Spirit of God, but wholly inspired. He is the whole man; total symbol and total reality. He alone can call God 'Abba', 'Father', he is God without remainder. In him there is no private precinct, no reserved area. He claims not likeness with the Father, but oneness. He does what the Father does; he loves totally. He is all giving, and all for giving.

Christ's work is to reveal God as Father and as our only future. Each one of us needs a future. Christ comes to reveal God as our only Father and this revises our understanding of things, of life and death, of man and women, of our origin and end, and of the meaning and mystery of the universe. Let us look at Christ as a person. Not first at what he says, but at what he is. Christ is a personality. His personality precedes his preaching. His being determines his doing. It is the same with us. What we say and what we do derive their value from what we are. Christ's person-

ality inspires his preaching and animates all his practice. Personality is the pearl of great price.

To discover what man ought to be look at Christ; he reveals man undeformed. And he discloses that man is born to live with others; he is not a solo artist. Christ is not the abnormal man; he is the norm, we the abnormal. He is the concentric, we are the eccentric; he is the true, we are the out-of-true. To define man or woman is difficult because there is such variety. In man and woman we see both nobility and degradation. Classic writers, seeking to define man, may award him a high valuation and speak in lyrics. Others despair of man. Is he angel or animal? Christ is the answer. He does not merely reveal what it is to be divine; he reveals what it is to be human. And he reveals that we are not human beings, but human becomings. That we are not born human; we become human. Or sub-human. The choice is ours, not God's.

Christ speaks to man in his becoming or unbecoming, in his condition of sadness, in his consciousness of sin. I have used the word 'sin', but I cannot define it. It is one of the undefinable words. One cannot dispense with it, but it is mystery. Christ must reveal what sin is, and isolate the virus that infects every human heart. It is too deep for human diagnosis. Each of us defines sin arbitrarily according to temperament, according to the conventions of the time, according to education or parentage. Some people see sin as legal infringement; some as moral failure. In some religions sin is ritual offence. But every person believes in something malign which he denotes as the great sin. The people to whom Christ was talking had their definition, not only of what sin was, but who was the sinner. A whole caste of people was defined as damned, beyond hope of rescue. They were rejected by men and named as rejected by God. They were the garbage of creation fit only for burning. They were many. And they were miserable.

Christ's revelation does not subscribe to this accepted reading of sin. He offends the pious both by his revelation of sin and his definition of righteousness. He declares that our consciousness of sin is false consciousness and that we must revise our assumption about sin and righteousness. What Christ declares, and what many of his hearers found offensive, was his insistence that sin is universal. The best are not exempt. He reveals that man is sinful in

his origin. Sin is not superficial; not a rash but a radical distemper. That it is not accident; that it is original; that it is not against the law or a code or a rubric. It is a flaw, a fault in man's composition. Sin is man's attempt to disown his origin. For his origin is in God and man resents this originality and seeks autonomy. This is the Adam-instinct in man; this is the originating sin. Man resents his condition as creature and would arrogate independence of the Creator. Adam is the creature envious of God, seeking to be God, seeking to define in his own terms what is good and what is evil. He resents subordination, saying 'Better to reign in hell than serve in heaven', to quote Satan in *Paradise Lost*. But man's only origin is in God. Man in sin lives on a stolen origin. He is off-centre. Having sinned and lost his centre, he sees reality from an angle, aslant, out of true. He still sees God, but not as his ground and centre of gravity. He sees God as over-there, over-against. He sees God as rival. He sees God as threat, as dicey and dangerous. God is penal and punishing. Below the rim of consciousness, man nurses a hidden hostility to God which he experiences as rage or anxiety.

Many people have a naive approach to sin. They tend to think they are sinners because at some point in their life they began to commit sin. Not so. I am not a sinner because I commit sins. I commit sins because I am a sinner. Sin lies in my self. It is separation from my origin, from my true hearth and home, from my true good and my true God. No man, woman or child can ever say, 'I am sinless.' Yet Christ by his person reveals this: that sin though universal is not necessary. The equation that to be human is to be sinful is not true. What Christ incarnates is the authentically human. And he is without sin. Sin is the sub-human element in me. Sin is the unholy, the inhuman in me. Sin is deflection from the human. Christ is the truly human because in him there is no alienation from his origin. 'I and the Father are one.' He is at ease with the Father; we are dis-eased. He is at one with the Father, we are at two with the Father. And this experience of separation from God is the source of our discontent.

The opening chord of the good news is that sin is not a terminal disease, not an incurable cancer. The whole of the Gospels, the music and melody of Christ's teaching, is that sin is not the prevailing wind in the world. Forgiveness is the first reality. Many good people may never achieve this liberation; they let sin-con-

sciousness become sin-obsession and they cannot know that joy so eloquent in St Paul, which he called the freedom of the sons and daughters of God.

Christ conveys what is hard to believe, that the sin in me is not decisive; that man can be reborn, restored to his origin and become one with the Father, become human by affiliation with the only human. 'You too can be one as I and the Father are one.' The man who said that used the pronoun 'I' and he is a man; he is our man, our symbol, our representative. He represents us to the Father and he represents the Father to us. He is the representative present among us. Nothing can separate us from his presence, not even the most shaming sin. This is the opening chord of the good news. He is one with the Father. He is one with humankind. Naturalized into Christ we return to our true origin and see God less as fear, more as Father.

This change is slow, and this change is so radical that Christ employs a startling metaphor. He calls it 'rebirth'. Baptism is the sacrament of the Fatherhood of God and it restores a lost relationship and gives a man, woman or child, a new stance and status, a new courage and confidence. Sinners though we remain, we are released from the greatest sin of all, the sin of not believing. Not believing that God accepts me even though I feel unacceptable. This is the sin that disables God; it is cold refusal.

Baptism does not add something to a man, it actualizes a capacity already there, and experienced as ache. Man is born to be reborn, but is unaware of this capacity without revelation. Nicodemus, a holy man, a law-abiding Pharisee, was a pious and unhappy man. Deeply religious people are often dissatisfied and cannot diagnose the source of their distress. Nicodemus kept the law, observed the minutiae of Jewish ritual. Yet he was aware of an emptiness, a feeling that his life, though pious, was pointless. He sensed in Christ a spirit bold and affirmative. He came to Christ in the night and asked his secret. Christ disclosed that his spirit is the Spirit of God and its power can recreate the lost and lonely soul. This Spirit he would release for all those willing to receive it.

Nicodemus did not understand. For the language Christ used is the language of symbol and most people remain illiterate in this tongue. The common reading of religion is literalist. The language of Christ is a language of symbol, of metaphor not of metaphysics.

There is power in Christ's words; there is beauty and colour and provocation. When Christ said to Nicodemus, 'Unless a man be born again', Nicodemus understood this grossly and his question was naive. The blending of water and spirit baffled Nicodemus as it baffles every diminished imagination. For most people have a low view of matter and see it as shoddy stuff. But God loves matter; he invented it. Matter is not impediment, nor is it disposable. We are one. Flesh is the agent and eloquence of spirit. Spirit cannot speak except through matter. Christ asked for a high estimate of matter. He did not think himself degraded when the Word was made flesh. He did not see himself as slumming. For Christ, creation is the music of the Creator, emblem of the quality of the Father, and of the creativity of the Spirit. The genesis of things begins with dead water. The Spirit imparts life to this sterility; water animated by the Spirit becomes the tonic of renovation. Man's re-generation comes by water and the Spirit. And deadness becomes life.

Sacrament requires perceiving eyes. It requires us to see things more deeply, even more poetically. The baptized are the twice-born; they stand on new ground and in a new relationship. With baptism the creator-creature relationship dies. This child is now a son or daughter. Baptism is the sacrament of the fatherhood of God, and every child born into this world is born for God. Birth cannot be manufactured by man, nor can baptism. God must make the first advance; man can only reply or refuse. Baptism is never compelled; it is offered. The child becomes a son or daughter, finds its true self. The sons and daughters of God have the Father for their security and the Spirit for their maturity. The baptized child is a kind of other Christ, no longer living in fear, but warmed by affection. This is the glory of baptism.

The symbolism of baptism is that of death and resurrection. It is a dying and a rising. To present baptism as a kind of mysterious washing of an invisible stain is a diminished understanding of this sacrament. Baptism is a real change. It is a change of consciousness. The fear-centred become the love-centred, Easter people, risen and renewed. Life is the key word in baptism and there is only one engaging symbol of life. It is growth. Man does not grow easily and effortlessly, like the tree in the orchard. Man grows only by a series of dyings and risings. The rhythm of all life, sacred and secular, is not linear, not ascent or descent. There is always

undulation. It is rise and fall, decay and renovation. That is the rhythm of baptism. The child is lowered into the water and dies to the life distanced from God and is raised to the life with God as Father. And baptism does not end at the font; it begins there. To see baptism as a once-for-all, something sealed by a certificate, is to misunderstand it. It initiates man into the rhythm of the Really Real. Naturalized into Christ man now reads all his experience from Christ's experience. And the teaching text is one sentence, 'He who would save his life will lose it.' That crisp assertion does not make sense unless we realize that the word 'life' is used differently in the beginning and at the end of the sentence. 'He who would save his life will lose it', is a contradiction unless we understand the two meaning of life. One must die to one life and it takes time; a life-time. A new life is born of this submission. Not egocentric but theocentric; God-centred. Not life apart from God but life with God. Life apart from God is sin and separation. Life with God moves into the green pastures of peace. 'My peace I give you.' First, in baptism. There a seed is sown.

Christ 'died' many times. Calvary was the climax of a play often rehearsed. When Christ was impaled on the cross, he could see the temple. The temple was the scenario of his first dying, of his first descent into hell. There he died to childhood, to the cosy world of the kitchen. Each must break emotionally with the parent, must die to dependence and be reborn, adolescent and adult. This involves hurt, necessary hurt. Baptism was born of hurt. Mary was pained by Christ's seeming neglect, and she did not fully understand. Christ had to make that emotional break in order to become his own man: a person, not an appendage.

Crisis comes when the child realizes that parents are not God, but weak and fearful. This is a real dying, a descent into hell. Christ broke with his parents in a bold action. He lost them for three days. He argued with the scribes. For three nights and days he was lost. He prayed, he suffered and he died. There he was reborn. He lost one life, the protected life, and he won another, a larger, more demanding life. He emerged with a new consciousness and with one luminous conviction: the exclusive fatherhood of God. This world was the Father's world; Christ's work was the Father's work.

Christ's next dying was death to a life not touched by temptation. The temptation is to abandon the Father, to question his

care and competence. It is to settle for humanism, and to live by a secular trinity, of power, prestige and possessions. This trinity is unholy but it does promise life with little demand. Its promise is bread. And 'bread alone' is the daily seduction. The theology of the market is an attractive theology. It is the catechism of the world, of commerce and accumulation. What matters is matter; the Good consists in goods. Christ knew this temptation and he died to the life made secure with Satan. He heard the whisper to renounce the Father and find an easier future. It reached its climax, as it did for Adam, in a garden. Here Christ was confronted with the one deadly decision: death or life. He sweated blood in confrontation with this question. The will to live was strong, and was in conflict with the grim image of death. He was young, he had a following. What should he do? The will of the Father was that he should persevere and die. But death usually looks like folly; life always appears as wisdom. He was offered a choice between life and death. He chose death; he got Life. This is the last baptism, and this the most painful. And the most fertile. We live on its holy and healing harvest.

Christ asked his disciples, when quarrelling about precedence in the Kingdom, an odd question. Did they understand it? He asked, 'Can you be baptized with the baptism which I am going to be baptized with?' He was talking about baptism very starkly. Baptism is not a once-for-all at the font; it is insemination. It must grow; and it grows not effortlessly, it grows by adversity and through those death-things that afflict us all. When our world falls apart, and seems to splinter, when life seems pointless and God is dead, then faith can grow, not under glass but in the fields of affliction.

Sacrament is dialogue. It asks one to give and one to receive. It is not magic, not mere ritual. There must be willingness. In each sacrament there must be expressed desire. If baptism is just something done then it is magic; the person is passive. But baptism is personal. It initiates man into the personal structure of reality. God is his Father, Christ is the way, and the Spirit of love is the force imparting confidence and cohesion. Baptism empowers, enables and energizes. And so we are baptized, in one name but in three powers. Name signifies power. In the name of the Father, who is our security. In the name of the Son, who is our way and our wisdom. In the name of the Spirit, who gives courage and

maturity. This is a new person, whose outlook on life, on people, on death, on love, on the world is changed. The symbol of baptism is total. It symbolizes the whole of the Christian economy: birth, dying and resurrection.

Yet, though baptism symbolizes everything, it achieves only something. Baptism is sowing. It has an element of reach, a forward movement and it looks to the future. It is a seed, but a seed needs water and nourishment. Baptism is incomplete. Baptism is baptism for. Baptism is for the Eucharist. Baptism demands bread if it is not to die of malnutrition. Baptism confers faith, but all faith is a green and growing thing. It needs divine nourishment and daily nourishment. A man is born once and needs only one baptism. Without the Eucharist we cannot fulfil our baptismal promise. Baptism is conferred in the presence of the community, parents, godparents, parishioners. Eucharist is meaningless without the real presence of Christ, there to be received. It is not good for man or woman to be alone, it is evil. Birth initiates a child into the people of God.

At the Easter vigil, a moving part of the service dwells on baptism. One action is the renewal of our baptismal promises. Why? Because we are human. We need to recall that baptism did not end the day we were baptized. Many people may not realize the promise inherent in their baptism. Baptismal moments confront us all. The child goes to school at the age of five and this is a critical moment. It sees the mother turn away for the first time, and leave it alone in a class-room with strange children and a strange teacher. The child cries. This is a moment of death. And a moment of life. Getting married, getting ordained, a new job, a new responsibility, all these are baptismal moments. All call for a response, a call for a 'Yes' or 'No'. Baptism is the seed which must die if it is to fruit and flower and bless the world with beauty. Real growth is growth in personality. It is evident in confidence. Confidence is simply two Latin words, *cum fide*. What the child receives at the font is its true self. Its gravity is in God, not in its own wayward capacity. We are always being asked, 'Are you willing to be baptized?' The answer is 'Yes' or 'No', faith or fear, death or fire.

But the option is ours.

4

SACRAMENTS OF RECUPERATION

The wheat-germ of Christianity is forgiveness. That is what makes Christianity Christian. Forgiveness cannot be caught in words nor cased in a definition. The sublime truths find no words to contain them; each eludes analysis. Forgiveness can only be experienced. The sublime things cannot be spoken; they can only be acted. When we speak of forgiveness we speak of God, for forgiveness belongs to God. To err is human; to forgive divine. God is the totally personal because he is totally for. For what? For giving. Man is most personal when he is a being for; for giving. Some confusion has blurred the meaning of the sacrament of reconciliation, and the world 'penance' and 'confession' lay the accent in the wrong place. They make man his own physician and impose the work of reconciliation on the sorrowing heart. This is a burden no man can sustain. If the burden is laid on me I am driven to desperation for I cannot be my own redeemer, only my own executioner.

How can I win forgiveness? I cannot. Forgiveness is the sweet juice of the gratuitous and the joy of the given. It cannot be bought by bribe or sacrifices. It is not the reward of a confession scrupulously made through species and number. That may minister to anxiety, and may diminish the role of God the reconciler.

Nor can we know forgiveness through our feelings. We cannot command our emotions and are not asked to. We cannot engender the tears of contrition, though we long to feel contrite. Forgiveness is of God. All we can do is receive it. This is our contribution. To desire it; to seek it and to receive it. But it is not purchase and we do not pay. We must receive it in humility and with thanksgiving. But it is divine donation, always mercy, never merit. For too many people sin is the presiding religious reality. Sin smears the horizon of existence and weighs on the consciousness night and day. Yet sin does not hold the supremacy. Christ's teaching opens with the word 'forgiveness': 'Your sins are forgiven; your faith

29

makes you whole.' At Mass we stand but do not say, 'We believe in sin.' We say, 'We believe in forgiveness of sins.' To believe in sin is common; to believe in forgiveness is Christian. And it is hard to believe in forgiveness; perhaps only the forgiven fully believe. Magdalen believed and there is joy in her demeanour and light in her eyes.

Forgiveness is the work of Christ and the work committed to the Church. The Church must not say it is a forgiving community, for shrill assertion does not ring true. The Church must be seen to be a forgiving community. Not a condemning community, nor a disapproving community. Its mood and manners must not be that of an excluding company looking coldly on the failures, and imposing iron conditions of return. The Church must be an open and accepting Church. Christ did not have to say his heart was full of forgiveness. It warmed the world like the rays of a summer sun. His life, his miracles, his parables, his deeds and his death proclaimed that he was totally on our side, totally for, totally forgiving. He did not deny that just being alive entailed a yoke and a burden. But 'My yoke is sweet, my burden light.' His work was not to make life grim, but to make it glorious. He was there to lift the burden, to carry the cross and to pioneer the path to the city and to salvation.

Forgiveness is not confined to the confessional. That is a visible sign of sorrow and true return to the community. St Thomas Aquinas writes, 'Most people who come to confession are already forgiven.' What, then, is the agent of forgiveness from our side? The true agent we name sorrow. And sorrow is not easy to understand. It can be confused too easily with negative and neurotic emotions.

Sin we partly understand. Sin causes pain, but why? It causes a deeper pain than any other affliction. The reason is that we do not entirely want to sin. St Paul expresses this in a classic line of lament: 'The evil which I will not, that I do.' the pain is the pain of interior conflict between two impulses. The conflict between what I will and what I can. There is a civil war inside me, a contest between two nouns; desire at war with capacity. And there is a hiatus between two verbs: between 'can' and 'will'. That is the root of sin and that is the source of our sadness. St Paul sees this with the sharp eyes of the prophet and the poet. He is able to articulate it in a language of great simplicity when he writes of his

30

pain; he cannot do what he wants to do. This is dilemma; this seems to make life an impasse. We are incompetent to do what we aspire to do. I want to be good and I am not good. This pain is world-wide. The pagans were troubled by this tragedy. A pagan poet inscribed a memorable line, *Video meliora proboque, deteriora sequor.* 'I see what is good and I approve; I do what is evil.' There again is the fault, the fracture, the gap between 'will' and 'can'.

All tragedy from Sophocles to Shakespeare explores this theme, and only because it must. Great drama is tragedy; not history, not comedy. For many people, life is experienced as tragedy and men and woman seek to explore it. Macbeth and Hamlet are tragic figures, outsize characters who take on God and defy his dominion. They disown their incompetence, deny that they are subjects, deny that they are creatures. Each seizes the sceptre of God and seeks to find salvation single-handed. Macbeth wants to be king. Kingship is an archetypal symbol of godhead. One sinful deed, the murder of Duncan, will bring Macbeth divinity and dispose of God and his supremacy. Yet, we have heard this story before. The witches in Macbeth predict Macbeth will be king; the serpent in the garden insinuated that Adam could be God. It is the eternal temptation. Many tragedies are variations on Genesis and Adam is everyman in his hostility to God, in his rejection of creatureliness.

Sin, then, lies deep. It is pain because it is incompetence and there is nothing we resent so much in ourselves as our incompetence. It hurts our pride. It is wise to think of sin in the singular because sin is singular. There is one radical sin. What we call sins are symptoms. They are the sores which reveal a poison in the blood. Sin is a disorder in me. And I want order; for order is peace and disorder is pain. The outcrop of the disorder in me is division. It divides me from me, and me from people, and me from the creator and the good things of creation.

Sin can be the sin of the group and this sin is wonderfully insidious. Notice how Christ addresses the Pharisees as a group. Among the Pharisees there were many people of admirable sanctity. But he locates a group-sin among them. It is wise to accept that a community, a school, a convent, a parish, a church, can be in sin. Group-sin is easily condoned by the community because a community, accustomed to the sin, is unaware of it. The Pharisees

31

could not see the sin Christ charged them with. It was clear to Christ and distressed him deeply. Sin is not only what you whisper in the gloom of the confessional. Real sin is seldom secret, seldom solitary. Real sin is patent, obvious and clear to people. Sin is often obvious to everyone except the sinner. Sin largely turns on the way I treat other people. The people near to me make the arena; the neighbour is the test. But casuistry can console by a sly redefinition of the neighbour. Casuistry grew like weeds in Christ's time but he would not be drawn into its sly distinctions. When asked the casuistical question, 'Who is my neighbour?' he evaded a casuist's reply. His life and death make inconvenient answer.

Christ does not see sin only as an individual act, done in the dark. He points to collective sin, to the sin of the sect. For the individual sinner Christ has tender words, for Magdalen, the publican, the repentant thief. Failure is not the danger. The admitted sinners, the bent reeds, the smoking flax confess their failure and receive forgiveness. The sin that dismays Christ is the sin of the group. Here he must use shock tactics and language of intensity, for the group can plate sin as gold and call it righteousness. Christ has to reveal, in metaphors of violence, that this group, so pious in its pretensions, is, in fact, sinful. It is the group that is recalcitrant to revelation; to the revelation of sin and of righteousness. For the group is creamed with complacency and each member reinforces the error of the other. Pope John restored the old title, 'A church of sinners', and calls the Church to look inward and to discover its concealed sin. Is the Church relaying the truth or a human polity? This is hard work and this is humbling work. And this is the work of the Spirit. The Church, as a community, must say each day, 'I confess.' The Mass wisely begins with a confession of failure. Each congregation is the Church in miniature, and before it dare speak the word of the gospel it must confess its sin and ask for absolution.

The priesthood is a group and the priesthood can have its own particular sin. A priest, in his preaching, can mislead, but he is called to lead. He is called to preach the good news; nothing else. He has no commission to air opinions, vent his prejudices, or preach a weird gospel of his own. 'Woe is me if I do not preach *the gospel.*' Anybody can preach. It is preaching the gospel that is hard. A priest must preach the good news and its light is the dawn of forgiveness. Christ is the luminous symbol and the sweet

agent of absolution. This must be preached, day in and day out, week in and week out, year in and year out. For it is so hard to believe. To believe in God is to believe that I am loved. Few easily accept that they are lovable and are loved unconditionally. Yet they are around; they are the salt of the earth and the light of the world. They are the people of God.

The man most resistant to the good news was the Pharisee. He is an interesting character because he is a pious man and he could not be faulted on law or morality. It is unwise to see the Pharisee as a conscious hypocrite. Most hypocrisy is not conscious; it must be uncovered. And painfully. This revelation provokes resistance for it hurts before it heals. Hurts our pride. This is the unkindest cut of all.

What, exactly, was this sin of the Pharisee and why so serious? It was simply, a conviction that by mere observance of the law in all its complexity he had achieved salvation without benefit of grace. He had levelled with God by a life of rigour; he asked for no redeemer. He could not recognize Christ for his eyes were proud, and his heart engrossed in his own excellence. He was not as the rest of men; sinful. The Pharisees were exempt from the universal taint. They saw themselves as a spiritual élite, an aristocracy of virtue in need of no repentance and asking neither God nor man for pardon or reprieve. Christ was superfluous; forgiveness an irrelevance.

Faced with this pride, Christ had to employ sharp weaponry if he was to save them from their illusion. Disillusion, though painful, is a way to the truth. It removes illusions. One potent weapon was the parable. The Pharisee and the publican is a parable of truth, distilled revelation from beginning to end. Two men disclose their hidden attitudes. And each is revealing himself, as do we all, through a prayer. Prayer is the best mirror of mind and heart.

The Pharisee reveals himself in a prayer which is spoken pride. Its pronoun is 'I'. 'I thank God that I am not as the rest of man.' This is the hidden lie. Yet an instinct in us wants to belong to an élite, and to find cover in the clique. Even the Church which is called to serve mankind can see itself as superior. Peter was appalled the night Christ wore the apron of the slave and did a menial deed. The Saviour washed the feet of the sinner. Strange revelation! And how easily resisted!

The publican is the admitted sinner drawn in profile. He too

reveals himself in a prayer, but it opens with the word 'Lord'. God alone is Lord, and him alone we address in prayer. 'Have mercy'. God is almighty only because he is all-mercy. Mercy on whom? On me. Why? Because a sinner. This is far from easy to accept. God loves us not because we are like him, but because we are unlike him. He loves us as we are and will lead us to where we want to be. The publican does not regress on himself or wax maudlin on his sins. His prayer is brief yet strong. Strong in faith; faith in forgiveness. Like so many he is despised by men but loved by God.

The genius of sin lies in its ability to find cover. Sin covers itself in pious disguise and the sinner is often his own best deceiver. Sin covers; revelation uncovers and we turn from its light. All Christ asks is for people to listen, to be open, to learn. In other words, to uncover, to confess. Sin says, 'I am not as the rest of men.' This is the master lie. This is cover. Repentance says, 'I confess, I uncover.' Christ says, 'Your sins are forgiven.' This is to recover, to put on Christ. And this makes the fine Christian crescendo. Covering, uncovering, recovering.

The opposite of sin is not virtue; it is faith. Unfaith disables God. So we pray after the Pater Noster; 'Look not on our sins, but on the faith of the Church.' Faith is larger than most of us imagine. It is more than assent to truths; that can diminish it to a thing of the mind. Perhaps a good word for faith is confidence. Faith never denies its own weakness. Yet it feels strong by a kind of given strength, and like the moon it lives on borrowed light.

The opposite of sin is faith. Christ sees the sinner as a loner, half-hoping for salvation without faith in God or man. A daily symptom of sin is anxiety. Christ's 'Be not anxious' is a serious imperative. So we pray after the Pater Noster, 'Free us from sin and keep us from all anxiety.' Anxiety is the cause of many actual sins. Were we perfectly at peace, sin would not find entry. Anxiety is a killer and Christ sees it as a great corrosive, sin's primary symptom.

The modern Catholic has a poor hold on sin, but has a strong sense of guilt. There is a difference. Guilt is sin experienced in isolation, detached from forgiveness. Guilt is introvert. It has very little faith. It does not know sorrow; only remorse. Remorse is acid; it eats at the arteries of the interior. Many good people are guilt-ridden, and confuse this with a sense of sin. Not so. The

publican had a strong sense of sin, and his prayer is rich in the protein of faith. Four strong words: 'Lord, mercy, me, sinner'.

Sorrow is quite different. Guilt is a loner; sorrow is a believer. Sorrow looks to the light and inhales the oxygen of forgiveness. Sorrow knows that no matter how great its sin the forgiveness of God is far, far greater. Sorrow does not dismiss the sins; nor does it dwell on it. It looks upward and outward and inhales the clean, resurrection air. It accepts God as the one who forgives, gladly, graciously and unconditionally. Sorrow leads to release and to recuperation. And the mood of sorrow is, simply, joy. 'There shall be more joy before the angels of God upon one sinner coming back than upon ninety-nine who do not need to.' How many believe that? How many of us associate the sacrament of re-conciliation with joy? Yet that is its mood and melody.

Both Judas and Peter betrayed Christ. Judas had no sense of sin because he had no sense of forgiveness. He was neurotically guilt-ridden. He tried to do everything alone; to delete his own sin and manufacture forgiveness. He took the money back, he took his own life. The wages of that sin, unfaith, is always death. Peter betrayed Christ through weakness, but a flicker of faith remained. His betrayal was not beyond the generosity of Christ. No sin is except unfaith.

Possibly only realized forgiveness leads us to light on the splen-dour of forgiveness. Forgiveness comes tax-paid and that is the difficulty; it is too good to be true. All that Christ asks for is faith. 'Your sins are forgiven.' And the kind corollary, 'Your faith has made you whole.'

Sin can be waste, opportunity missed and talent unused. Each of us has one talent, personality. So much in life turns on its employment. In one parable Jesus presents the two options open to us. One man uses his talent, makes it grow and fructify, and on his return is applauded. The other plays it safe, takes no chances; he buries his talent. There is no increase. No addition. He is reproved for his sin. But what sin? The sin is opportunity missed. And opportunity is presented to all, though we blame circumstance, bad parentage or bad luck. Yet these are pretexts. The true cause is fear, want of faith. The man or woman of faith makes opportunity, is unafraid of risk and makes living an adven-ture, not a moan. It is good to see sin negatively; as life refused. The Greek word for sin means missing the mark. We all have

opportunity and each of us is blest with one gold talent. Why do we bury it? The answer is spoken in the parable, 'Sir, I know thou art a hard man.' That is; God you are a hard god. He is oppressed by the fear of God; one cannot have faith in a god of stone. And without faith there can be no ignition.

Sin is the child of fear. 'Fear not' is one of Christ's admonitions. Fear must die in the arms of forgiveness. In time we shall recover its true mood and meaning. The Church is called to relay forgiveness, and the sacrament of reconciliation is a healing sacrament for we are all sinners, all walking wounded. And there are moments when temptation against faith becomes acute. Such an occasion is illness. Illness comes to all; the danger resides in not seeing it as Christ saw it. Christ sees sickness as evil, something to be fought, something to be overcome. There is temptation to see sickness as a means of self-indulgence. The hypochondriac uses sickness to bring exemption from the stress of things, and to lay burdens on those seeking to help and heal him.

The sacrament of the sick reveals that sickness is evidence of evil in the world. Not moral evil; it is just there like cancer and scars the body of humankind. But sickness is evil and is to be overcome. To Christ it is something to be fought. The sacrament of the sick is, itself, a sacrament of recuperation and return to life; it is for return to health and the community. For Christ, forgiveness of sins and cure of disease were closely allied. The man who seeks the sacrament of the sick must be a man of faith. He must see his illness as something to be overcome, and dearly want to overcome it. But he needs strength, and oil is the classic symbol of the Spirit as strength. It sacramentalizes the life-wish; the life-wish of Eucharist and for community. Anointing points to the Eucharist and to life, not to despair and dissolution.

The correct response to illness is not resignation. Christ never counselled a pale acquiescence. Even if the illness is mortal and we know the person will die, then let him have faith that the life to come is Life indeed. A fatalistic surrender is not the Christian attitude. Christ cures the sick, casts out demons and forgives sins. These are closely related. Faith in God is faith in healing.

St James writes, 'Let him bring in the priests of the Church.' The sick man seeks to be restored to health and to the community. And this desire is an act in God and a mark of health. This is wholesome and this is Christian.

36

Christianity is about forgiveness, and forgiveness is more than cancellation. Forgiveness is a total thing. A person is a forgiving person, or an unforgiving person and, as Catholics, we are members of a forgiving Church. And the message we must relay to the world is that in spite of all the death-things, inflation, war, destitution, there is a stronger presence and a holy power on this planet. And the stronger presence and person has only one sentence to sustain us in sadness and sin: 'Your sins are forgiven, your faith makes you whole.'

5

THE BREAD OF THE BAPTIZED

The baptized are a body of people naturalized into Christ. They seek to live not in isolation, but in true communion with God and people. They live as members of a body; not loners but lovers. This manner of life is not easy. Unaided, it is impossible. Baptism is not fulfilment; no one can live on baptism. For baptism is a birth and the born need bread. Christ's manifesto 'I am the bread of life', is no metaphor. It is meat and has meaning. It imparts the meaning of life and of all things that matter.

For the Catholic the Eucharist focuses everything. This is not easy or obvious. Christ's revelation of the Eucharist is given in St John's Gospel and what is conspicuous about this occasion is its rejection. The first sermon on the Eucharist met failure. The first sermon on the Eucharist met refusal. Either they could not understand or they could not accept. Most of Christ's contemporaries could accept baptism; few could accept Eucharist. We seek the reasons for this resistance.

First, it seems that many pious people prefer isolation; isolation lowers demand. Religion becomes private; I and God in quiet conclave. Prayer is secrecy; conduct an observance of laws. Other people must not intrude and a pride proclaims that the pious keep themselves to themselves. They accept, sincerely accept, one half of Christ's command, 'Thou shalt love the Lord thy God.' They do not accept its corollary, 'Thou shalt love thy neighbour as thyself.' Exclusion is strong in many people. Indeed, the story of the Tower of Babel is revealing. And this temptation persists; to seek God by straight access, by hard and lonely endeavour. It is the spirituality of the loner, and this spirituality is eager for God, but cool on people. The consequence of the story of the Tower of Babel is discord, loss of shared life and language. They cannot build the tower and they cannot converse. Each has his own language and they learn that this is not the way; a private pursuit is not the answer. The Tower of Babel is an unfinished building.

We cannot live except by communication, not merely with God, but with people. Yet individualism is natural; it is communion that makes the demand. Christ offers the hand of communion, but human instinct declines to take it. To receive asks for a new heart if a man is to accept this invitation. He must receive a new spirit.

At Pentecost people speaking different languages understood the preaching of the apostles because the Spirit of God renewed them. And there is only one Spirit. The Holy Spirit speaks the same language to all people, and enables all to open to God and to the neighbour. But many do not want to receive this Spirit; they prefer to be alone. Pentecost reverses Babel. At Babel they could not understand each other. At Pentecost people of different tongues could understand the apostles, for this was the Spirit speaking a universal vernacular.

Communication begins with a new literacy which is the language of Christ. It takes a life-time to learn. But why is this so? The life and language of Christ are the life and language of sacrifice. And sacrifice is an elusive word. It has acquired a somewhat bleak inflection, and seems to run counter to the divine and melodious word which is 'love'. Love suggests ecstasy, but sacrifice is a wintry word. Men and women want fulfilment but sacrifice seems to entail destruction. So the language of Christ is hard to understand because love and sacrifice appear to be incompatible. Yet Christ's life is a blend of love and sacrifice, of beauty and severity.

What, then, is sacrifice? One approach is to turn to the Old Testament and to a story which seems to be barbaric. It is the story of Abraham and Isaac. Abraham is the figure of faith. To the Jew, Abraham is all a good Jew should be. He obeys without question. And the gleam in Abraham's eye is his son, Isaac, for he loves Isaac to distraction. Isaac is his jewel and his joy. And his future. Abraham will live on through Isaac and his posterity. What a rare love burns there. And how cruel when God commands Abraham to sacrifice Isaac, to destroy him. This sword will not destroy Isaac only. It will destroy Abraham for Abraham's attachment to Isaac is total, his love of Isaac is his life. Here is one of the strangest stories and one not easy to accept. It is a story with a sharp point and well worth pondering because this story is not rational. It is distilled revelation.

Isaac did not die. There was no immolation, no death, no

destruction. Yet, there was sacrifice. Sacrifice is not some thing. Sacrifice is some one. It is the personal. On that raw morning Isaac does not die; Abraham does. Abraham dies to a love of Isaac which was possessive for he did not see Isaac as a person but as an appendage. Abraham did not see Isaac as unique but as his replica. So, if Isaac was to live and to grow and to be and to become, Abraham had to let him go. Abraham had to let him be; let Isaac be himself. This is sacrifice. And this is love. Abraham died and died painfully to a love that was imperfect because possessive. And Abraham rose to a love that no longer confined Isaac and no longer confined himself. Abraham's sacrifice was not a negative thing. He said 'Yes' to God when every instinct in him cried out to say, 'No, I want my son.' He gave his son away. This sacrifice was made in faith and was wonderfully fertile. It reveals love at its most intense, and at its most pure; love as the creative thing. By unconditional surrender, Abraham did not lose a son; he lost a satellite. By surrendering Isaac, Abraham gained a son and lost a servant. Isaac was born of a sacrifice. Born free, a person, no longer a possession.

This is an instructive story and reveals the wonder of personality. To whom does Isaac belong? To Abraham? No. To God? No. Isaac belongs to Isaac. For God is the one who lets me be. Be myself. God does not compel or coerce. God invites, persuades, attracts, calls. But he does not impose. Each one of us is free to say 'Yes' or 'No' to God. God is the one who lets me be. And God is the one who asks me to let the loved one be himself or herself. It is at this point we begin to understand both the meaning of love and the meaning of sacrifice. True love is uncompelled. It is not forced. The dissolvent of love is possession. God does not possess me; he lets me be. If God possesses, then we are pawns. If God owns us, we are servants. It is Christ's first work to set us free, to call us not servants but friends, not retainers but a family of sons and daughters. God is the freedom that creates other freedoms. The central and saving truth is that God does not compel or force or frighten me. God loves me. To apprehend that is, indeed, to see all things differently. The world is lit with glory.

And if God loves me, what should be the consequence? One sentence in St John is interesting because it seems to end the wrong way. It says this, 'If God so loves us'. Now one would expect the second half of that sentence to be, 'So shouldn't we

love God?', but it does not. It ends, 'If God so loves us then should not we love each other?' And it is St John above all who sees the command to love self, neighbour and God as one converging love. Love is indivisible. The one test of my love of God is earthed in the way I treat other people. 'If God so loves us should we not love each other?' This is the Christian disclosure, the new wine not to be held in old and porous wine-skins. Here we may begin to understand the Eucharist. For sacrifice is not one incident in Christ's life. Christ's life itself was sacrificial from the crib to the cross. That is why it was so happy. That was the secret of its creativity. Life without sacrifice lacks purpose, lacks expansion, is lonely and loveless. People may seek to live life without any giving; such a life will be mean and morose. God is giving God and does not shy from sacrifice.

The true rhythm of life must be revealed; the natural rhythm is uneven. 'My ways are not your ways. My thoughts are not your thoughts.' We need to be schooled to know why we resist so much of what Christ says. Christ's insistent call is to change. He sees change as the hinge of the Christian condition. His imperative is, 'Repent and believe': change and believe. Belief is not effortless; it is a child of change.

The call to change is far from congenial. Indeed, this call of Christ's to change was to cost him his life. A fear of change is deep in us all. Sameness is a sedative and seduces all but the brave. Christ's call to change was offensive to many pious ears. So it remains. Intransigence is armour for the timid heart and may call itself loyalty. But it is fear in disguise. Christ did not merely preach change. He enacted it. We only half-hear what Christ is saying unless we read the signs. And the signs can be so easily misunderstood.

The Jews, like every nation, believed in a golden age. Unlike other nations the Jews saw the golden age, not in the past, but in the future, and looked forward to this millennium. Being human, they conceived it politically, with the Jews as the master-race and the Gentiles as slaves. They believed in a golden age but they did not use the symbol 'gold'. For the Jews the symbol was wine. The golden age for them was the wine age. Wine was fullness. The imperfect age in which they lived was the water age. Water symbolized the imperfect; the colourless, the incomplete. Wine stood for the rich, and realized kingdom. So when at Cana in Galilee

41

Christ changed the water into wine, this was an historical action. A sign. The Jews knew their history, they knew their Scriptures; they knew what Christ was claiming. He was claiming and proclaiming that he was to inaugurate the new age; claiming to be the one who was to come, who was to make a definitive change and to bring fulfilment. The message of Christ was spoken through the alphabet of sign and sacrament. What happened at Cana was not merely an act to relieve an embarrassed host. And what happened at Cana was not primarily an exhibition of power. This is to misunderstand miracle.

Miracle is not the sensational, designed to impress or to prove. Miracles are not there to prove anything. Miracles are there to reveal. Miracle and parable do the same thing. They are revealing the truth. Miracle is misunderstood if presented as proof; miracle is understood if presented as revelation. Christ himself said that miracles do not prove anything. At the end of the parable of Dives and Lazarus, he is emphatic that even if someone were to rise from the dead, people will not believe.

Cana is a revelation that Christ will pave the way to the Kingdom, to the wedding of man with God. Man has devised a variety of approaches to God, through philosophy, through the law or through magic. Christ declares these to be blind alleys. God is the personal and can only be reached through the person, but the person must symbolize and be present. Christ is the person who symbolizes God completely. Christ is God in the flesh, God sacramentalized, God made accessible. So Christ is unswerving in his statement that he will be accessible to all through the genius of symbol and the glory of sacrament.

The change of water into wine is an action which reveals that there is no life without change. Everyone wants the life of wine and roses, and God will provide the wine as he provides the roses. But the new wine requires new wine-skins. There lies the resistance; we want new wine, but we want the tried ways and the old wine-skins. Christ sees this as impossible. We too must be changed, as water is changed into wine. And throughout his life, Christ intensifies the image and symbol of the wine. In his autumnal days, Christ speaks with a cadence that comforts and consoles. Let us take note of what he says, because the language is more than poetry. It is sacramental. 'I am the vine, and you are the branches.' What does this mean? No prophet had ever spoken

like this, no philosopher, no theologian, no teacher, 'I am the vine, you the branches.' The metaphor is deeply personal; the life of the vine and of the branches is one. One juice imparts life to both. Christ is speaking of an intimacy between God and man that exceeds expectation. Here we enter the sanctuary of sacrament. The question occurs, as it occurred in his audience; 'How can this man give us his flesh to eat and his blood to drink?' It is a good question; there is only one answer. Through sacrament. For the final change is not water into wine; that was physical. The final change is wine into blood. Life-blood. And that is sacramental. The final change is not chemical; the wine remains as a sign but the reality is the pulse and person of Christ; real and realizing.

The presence of Christ in the Eucharist is not physical. It is more. It is personal. This presence is more vivid, more vitalizing than physical presence. The Christ who wined and dined in Galilee could give to those who sat at table his words and his wisdom, and could relay new hope to those who broke bread with him. But this giving was incomplete; this communion was limited. There was a distance between them. Christ in the flesh could communicate only partially. Christ, raised and renewed, could impart his life totally. The price of Eucharist was a change: a death. This is the greatest change of all. Christ died to the life of limitation, to life enclosed by this too, too solid flesh. He was raised, immortal, imperishable, to life beyond restriction. This Christ we receive in the one way available, through the genius of sacrament.

There is a gradation of symbols. I use this word 'symbol' because it is a necessary word. For communication is through signs and symbols. But there is a gradation of symbols, from the simplest gesture, the smile or the handshake, to the most spectacular ritual. Ritual is symbol writ large. It conveys meaning. But even the simplest 'Thank you' is a sign, something sacramental.

Everyone seeks to give and receive love and the agent of communication is the sign. All love is a giving and a giving away; this we call sacrifice. Notice how Christ's ministry begins with change and culminates in transformation. On Calvary he gives himself away totally. For he alone is totally himself, the real and rounded personality with no reserved area. He is the totally human being because totally divine; the universal man. Nothing in Christ is for Christ. He is totally for. We are partially for. We have not his

capacity for giving. Christ does not die for his family or for his nation or for a political cause. Christ dies for what? For the world. To impart to it the means whereby it can find release from its sorrow and its sin. Unless we see Christ as totally for us, as the liberator, the tremendous lover, we miss the point of Calvary, of resurrection and of Eucharist. The death on Calvary is how Christ speaks his regard for humankind.

But, how can this love be conveyed? How can this forgiveness be received? How can this release be realized? There is no answer except sacrament. It can be dispensed as the spiritual must be dispensed, through visible things which give invisible fire.

The most evocative symbol of shared love is the meal; an indispensable symbol. The meal is wonderfully creative, creative of community. The meal is a gesture of acceptance and an agent of transformation. Here the lonely find company, the silent become articulate and the despondent recover joy. At the meal the dead come to life; discord and dissension die.

The Mass is a sacrificial meal. For here the love of Christ is communicated through signs of love. In the Mass symbol and reality are one. In baptism we receive the power of Christ; in Eucharist we receive the person of Christ. Nothing less will answer the ache of the heart. The Eucharist, then, is Christ; it is both in time and beyond it. Eucharist remembers the past, it makes present the Life, and it looks to the future, to that meal when all make one Body. We receive the real Body of Christ to build the body of mankind.

It is a mistake to see the Mass as remembrance of something past. The Mass is remembering the past but making present the Christ. It is also looking to the future. Catholics are sometimes accused of having no theology of the future, of merely wringing their hands and predicting calamity. That was not Christ's way. The Eucharist is looking to the future until he comes. Another error is to see the Eucharist as for me. But the Eucharist is not for me but for us. Sin manifests its violence in division but love manifests its glow in communion. Death is sin proclaiming its power to destroy. But Calvary is past. Christ died once and for all. But Easter is contemporary. We receive the risen Christ. He Easters in us and slowly we become Christified, by his real presence, by our receiving the food of our future.

The Eucharist is the sacrament of the future. And therefore the

44

Eucharist is the sacrament of challenge. The Eucharist challenges me to become what I am born to become, a son not a servant, one living in hope not in dread, believing that my sadness and my sin are not invincible. So it is wise always to see the Eucharist as a standing challenge to us all. The Eucharist can be presented in an anaemic form. One can see it as personal nourishment or individual medicine. One can speak of 'my Mass' and 'my communion', but that is to betray the message of the sacrament. It is to remove from the Eucharist that element of challenge and its call to change. The price of the Eucharist was high, for the price was dying. Christ changed totally, died and was raised. Through the Eucharist Christ speaks his challenge to all of us who believe or half-believe. But the resistance to change stays strong. The resistance may pose as humility. That is not the real resistance. The real resistance is always the same. It is unfaith. It is the refusal to believe that with God all things are possible, that his sacrifice is more potent than my sin. Christ invites all to the meal and, as the Gospel reveals, many do not come. They look for other paths and a smaller kingdom.

Peace makes the theme of the Mass after the Pater Noster, and pure peace is a given thing and can be received only by an asking heart. Peace is present when I accept myself as accepted by God even though I feel unacceptable. It is hard to believe in a God who does not make conditions or ask for payment. Yet he does not ask for worthiness, only for willingness. 'Lord I am not worthy' is a statement of fact. 'Say but the word' a statement of faith. Then we can come and eat.

But faith may be mere mood and a true faith must feed on action. The Mass is the action which re-presents, in its finest sense, the event and the person of Christ. History could not hold Christ and he is with us always, not as a dead hero, but alive and available to all who believe and come home to commune with one who is life and seeks only to impart it. The Christian tense is the present, continuous tense and the real presence is secured through sacrament. But presence is not for presence but for communion. It is God who makes the offer. 'The Body of Christ.' It is we who make reply, 'Amen'. Here sacrament touches the sublime when God and humankind meet and marry.

The Mass ends with a command, with three kind and courteous valedictions. Each contains the same verb 'go'. And each contains

the same noun, 'peace'. This makes every Christian a missionary. He is to go out. Go where? To the world. Go why? To love and serve the Lord. How? Through serving and saving any people. What do people really want? They want peace. Peace within their hearts, peace within their homes, peace to warm the world. 'Go in peace to love and serve the Lord.' A new commandment.

Christ says, 'Blessed are the peace-makers', never blessed are the peace-lovers. Peace-lovers are easy to find but peace-makers are the salt of the earth. There are few who, wherever they go, bring peace into a company. Yet that is what the Eucharist charges us to do. What we have received we are called to share. We have received the life and are asked to impart it in all its variety, as joy, as kindness, as life and enlargement. The test of the Mass is what we do after it. That 'go out' determines the point of the Mass. 'Go in peace to love and serve the Lord.' It is the echo of that great assize recorded in St Matthew when he describes in memorable language the interrogations of the last judgement. The key question is simple but surprising. 'I was hungry, did you give me to eat? I was thirsty, did you give me to drink?' Our question is 'When did I see you thirsty?' Then a strange answer. 'If you did it to the least of these little ones, you did it to me.' Christ is present in all. He hungers with the hungry and asks us to provide bread. To serve God is to serve people. Love is unselective.

Love of God is sacramentalized through love of those near to us, love of people. And love of the other is difficult; indeed impossible. But with God all things are possible. In communion we are with God. We receive his peace, and his person. We cannot live on our own resources for they are meagre rations. We can live on what we receive, the given love of Christ. And what we received we are called to give to a needy world. The Mass, which begins with an admission of weakness, 'I confess', ends with a command of strength, 'Go in peace to love and serve the Lord.' And the Lord lives in every hungry heart.

6

SACRAMENT AND MAGIC

The world we inhabit is a world of things. Cars, carpets, machines. These things are good and within the reach of gold. Gold is the oldest symbol of power over things. It awards real power, and its glitter seduces men to see its power as total. Gold is the secular and the best symbol of secular success. We live under persuasion to see it as the god who delivers the goods. Gold becomes divine; the finite becomes the infinite, the secular becomes the sacred. And if god is money, then we must live on accumulation. The good man is the millionaire. Gold is magic.

The world which sees the thing as all that matters is the world of magic. Magic is an outlook on life. It is more than trickery. Fork-bending is magic reduced to a game. But there is a serious magic which attracts us all, and we are only half-aware of its persuasions. Its power resides in its reticence. We experience magic in daily life, and a common assault comes through advertisement. The world of the advertiser is now a sophisticated world, with its schools and colleges and its experts. There is honest advertisement; direct description; the hard sell. There is dishonest advertisement and this appeals to a subconscious faith in magic. Even the best are conned.

What, then, is magic? Magic is that power which promises release from human distress by finite means. Magic promises what Christ promises, life and far larger life. Magic denies the sacred and does not take the human condition seriously. It cannot handle the big things like life or liberty or love. It pretends to manage life and it makes a promise; instant salvation by finite means. The advertiser insists that this car or this carpet will be more than a utility. It will change your life, make you a being apart, make you the envy of your unfortunate neighbours. It will give you confidence, make you a new person, and release you from the daily diet of adversity. Above all, it will release you from the pain of human experience.

Everyone says, 'I am not fooled by advertisements.' But the advertiser knows his work and our weakness. It was the advertiser who sold thalidomide to the medical profession. It is the advertiser who sells poor quality bread as good. He presents on television, not the bread, but a rural scene in a summer valley in the Cotswolds, accompanied by sweet and soothing music. This is the soft sell. It says nothing about the product. It sells by association of something beautiful with something inferior. It is fraud made art.

To say one is not influenced by advertising reveals that magic makes appeal to the subconscious. We are dupes of the hidden persuaders, because they skilfully dissemble. Magic builds on a false reading of reality which is in us all; untrue but attractive. How does it attract? By immediacy. It promises instant salvation. It sees salvation in the finite, in the thing, in what you can buy. It does not stay entirely in the field of the secular, but devises rites and rituals, has its priests, its fortune-tellers and its ceremonial. It sees in a stone, a charm, or an incantation a power that the finite does not have but pretends to have. So the charm is not just a brooch; it is a lucky charm. What is it appealing to? It is not appealing to faith because faith respects reason. It appeals to credulity. And credulity is the irrational. Never think that the first enemy of faith is scepticism. Not so. The most potent enemy of faith is credulity. And most people are credulous. Every con-man would endorse this assertion. Most people are conned, because most people are credulous.

Magic is a religion and we call it superstition. It is the cult of the secular posing as the sacred. And what attracts men and women to magic and superstition is the sheer harshness of reality; its rawness. Life can press too heavily, anxiety can exceed our capacity to contain it. Fears and phobias can lead to depressions too dark to endure. And promise of release from the rough of things makes people seek easy and instant escape. For example, from illness. The quack doctor commands a large clientèle. The quack medicine makes fortunes for the manufacturer. And the quack religion, no matter how eccentric, finds devoted adherents, only because it promises swift salvation.

But magic does not fulfil what it promises. Even primitive peoples questioned the claims of the magician. The story of Midas is an anti-magical story. Midas, you may remember, is awarded the gift of transmuting anything he touches into gold. This prom-

ises salvation at a touch. Nemesis enters when he touches his daughter and she is no longer his deeply-loved daughter, but a golden figurine. He has lost his most precious person, the leading love of his life. His nights and days are now pointless and deprived. All he has is gold. And all he wants is his daughter. A memorable story, and a tragic story. It is a pagan critique of magic.

Gold is the symbol of the impersonal god, and magic is the cult of the impersonal. The true God is personal and Christ is the presence and power of the personal. Reality is so hard. Magic seeks to evade reality by manipulation of the finite. Christ does otherwise. He seeks to lead men into reality, into the true, and he empowers them to contend with it. He does not deny that the cross is hard and heavy. He does not deny that the cross cannot be carried. Take up your cross and follow me through the valley to heaven and the heights.

How then does Christ see the finite? He has a true regard for the finite and a tender love of common things. When he becomes man he accepts the limitations of the finite and is fleshed in weakness. But he does not see the finite as magic sees the finite. Magic sees the thing, the object, as closed, as self-contained, as nothing but thing. This is the majority vision. But it is restricted vision, and sees the world as a warehouse, an emporium of utilities, a market of manufacture. Christ's vision is penetrating and he sees through the finite to the infinite, through the secular to the sacred. The finite is not self-sustaining; the world is not self-explanatory. The question Christ is answering is the question 'Why?'. This is the key question. Why reality? Why existence? Why the world? Why people? Why life? Why death? These are the big questions and these are the questions Christ is answering. Magic evades the question 'Why?'; it will not allow anyone to ask it. Magic deals only with the question 'What?'. Then it quietly attributes preternatural power to the natural thing. It opts to live on charm, not on virtue.

There are two visions of reality and each of us moves between them both. Christ's vision is sacramental. He does not deny that the finite has value in itself. Bread is nourishment. Wine exhilarates, oil is an emollient, water renews. Yet, Christ sees bread as something in its own right yet significant of a finer nutrition. This bread he calls living bread. Christ sees water as indispensable

to daily living, but he sees water also as significant of renewal and a finer regeneration.

Sacrament begins with vision, and it asks for eyes that see the sacred through the secular. To understand sacrament we need an imaginative shift, and some resist this vision and reduce the sacrament to magic and adroit manipulation. Magic is the mystique of materialism. It sees matter as the only reality and the whole world as walled by the material, a compound of clay.

Diminished vision is natural to man. It is the market vision, and its thesis asserts that the good is the useful. This assumption has seeped into the subconscious of the West and tempts us all. Life is dominated by economics; salvation comes through productivity. The balance of payments is the key to the kingdom and man and woman are valued by their wage. Once the wage becomes the idol of worship, man himself is a utility, a hand, no longer a heart.

The principle of utility was made into a philosophy by a man of genius and compassion, Jeremy Bentham (1748–1832). There was much truth in his philosophy and it brought amelioration to the poor and deprived living in squalor. But its assumption was materialist; that the good is the useful. Some saw the fallacy and voiced their protest. The character Gradgrind in *Hard Times* by Dickens is the utilitarian in caricature. Only the fact matters, the real is the useful. Wordsworth, a contemporary of the utilitarians, was saddened by this philosophy for it would exclude fair acres of reality; painting, poetry and religion. These do not subscribe to the principle of utility, and cannot be costed. Grace comes duty-free.

In three lines, Wordsworth pitied and impaled the utilitarian when he wrote:

> A primrose by a river's brim
> A yellow primrose was to him
> And it was nothing more.

There he presents two visions. The primrose is useless, unless it can be turned into gold and sold for cash. This dim and depressing vision has infected the West and desacralized its world. And this myopia makes sacrament difficult to understand, and can make liturgy drab and mechanical. Preaching loses power to uplift and transform. R. E. becomes the problem-child of education and few are willing to engage in it. This is the entail of a non-sacramental

view of things, and makes the world weightless. But the need for the sacred never goes away; it is deep in man, and it remains insistent. Man will always seek the sublime or will find some counterfeit. In magic. The magic of money, the mystique of materialism.

Christ found that materialism was an impediment to his message. People read reality mainly in materialist terms. The miracle of the loaves was not understood, because it was seen un-sacramentally, as new magic. It had no meaning apart from providing instant answer to a physical need. Christ regretted this deeply, and sought to convey that the miracle was not magic, but amazing grace, and a revelation of God as the single source of supply, of a finer loaf to make a finer bread.

Christ saw bread both as thing and as symbol. The people saw bread only as thing because their outlook was closed in matter. The miracle which is revelation was to them magic. The magic is materialism in sacred disguise.

Another instance; the story of the woman at the well. Throughout this story Christ and the woman are at cross-purposes. Two visions collide, two views are in conflict; the sacramental and the secular. It is a classic confrontation, because it plays on the theme of sacrament. Christ asks the woman a favour: 'Give me a drink.' He continues, 'If you only know what God is offering and who it is that is saying to you, 'Give me a drink', you would have been the one to ask and he would have given you living water.' Christ moves into a sacramental language. He speaks of a finite thing, water, and prefixes it with the adjective 'living'. Notice the woman's materialist rejoinder. 'You have no bucket, sir, and the well is deep. How could you get this living water?' That is a too human comment. Christ persists and stays with the language of sign and sacrament. He points to the well. 'Whoever drinks this water will get thirsty again. But anyone who drinks the water that I shall give will never be thirsty again. The water that I shall give will turn into a spring inside him, welling up to eternal life.' This is the grammar of sacrament. Real life is more than biology. It is interior. The heart is the altar of consecration.

Yet we can forgive the woman's obtuseness and her inability to understand. Because for her, as for the world, water is finite, a fluid for physical life. Christ also sees water as finite and necessary to common life. But man's real need is deeper. His thirst is for

51

life within, for a life of peace and expansion. It is this spirit every man, woman and child seeks. But this spirit cannot come to man except through matter, through wine and water.

Christ sees the finite, then, not as a closed reality but as open and as an agent of the infinite. This is to take the finite seriously. A primrose by a river's brim is not merely a yellow thing. It has beauty. What is beauty? It is not a frill hung on the rough cloth of things. Beauty is necessary; it is truth speaking to the eye. A primrose or a painting, a symphony or a sonnet are beautiful. Precious but not to be priced. One cannot find the one thing necessary even in the most pricey shops.

The best art is sacramental. It has no function other than to reveal the truth through finite agencies, through paint, or perfume, or sound, or style, or shape or structure. Magic has little time for beauty. Magic is functional. Its aim is pragmatic; to release man from the pains of being human, and to bring him luck, health or healing, without recourse to God or grace. Magic sees all power in the thing, in the brooch or diamond. It may believe in the gods of power, but always as loveless, and often as hostile and dangerous. But the gods can be manipulated by sacrifice or charm, for they too are finite, superhuman, never divine.

Magic comes easily to man because he lives in a world of things. And because sacrament employs the finite it is tempted to flirt with magic. Pure Christianity is good, red wine, but can be soured by superstition.

The health of the Church is in ratio to its sacramental insight. When the Church is in decay magic may intrude on sacrament. But the Church at its best has a sure grasp of sacrament and a sober, sacramental theology. Then the Church is alive and speaks through the beauty of its liturgy. The Church can best be judged by its liturgy and by its preaching. Beauty and truth: these are the twin lamps of liturgy and preaching. For most people the main encounter with God is the Sunday liturgy. During six days of the week they may never hear the name of Christ spoken, except in blasphemy. But what they come to Church for is the True. And truth is not a theory but a person. 'I am the truth.' This is the decisive equation. 'I am the truth.' But Christ cannot be personally received except in sacrament. The Mass is an action; something done. The Mass is not fixated on elements: it is a sacred action.

From beginning to end the Mass is conveying that there is a life

beyond work and worry. Christ gives meaning by giving himself, body, soul and divinity. And this truth cannot be conveyed in words. Indeed, the great truths can never be conveyed in words; they can only be acted and the Mass is the singular action. And so the Mass must not be performed perfunctorily, for beauty is truth's elocution; beauty of speech, of song and movement. Every gesture must be reverent and revealing. If the Mass is presented hastily or in a slovenly fashion or inaudibly there may be a sub-conscious conclusion that the Mass has no meaning, that the Mass is magic, a mime without much meaning. In magic, power resides in the ritual. Sacrament goes beyond the ritual and reaches a higher reality. It imparts a power exceeding ritual power. This power is the power of the person, the Christ, present, really present and inviting communion. Magic is essentially the rite. Sacrament goes beyond the rite; it makes present the living God. Faith in Christ brings men to Mass. Not faith in the rite. Faith in Christ is fortified by the Mass. Magic requires faith only in the rite. Mass requires faith in the person and the presentation must lift man above the rite to the reality that transcends it. Hence 'Sursum corda', 'Lift up your hearts.' Hence the elevation of the Host to symbolize its transcendence. Hence the elevation of people who commune with Christ and are freed from the tyranny of the trivial. They are christified by Christ and go away in peace. A rare peace; the peace of the Lord.

Men want the real. The Eucharist does not merely present the real in some metaphorical manner. Christ is realized. This is the genius of sacrament and this the force in symbol. The handshake does not feign reconciliation; it realizes it; seals it. In the Eucharist symbol and reality are one. The bread and wine are changed into the Body and Blood of Christ. The person of Christ is fully present, fully realized to be fully received. But, because we are immersed in the material we are subject to the temptation to magic. There is always a danger of making the elements separate things, magic things. This becomes evident in fear of touching the Host with the teeth or dropping the Host on the floor. These fears betray a semi-magical understanding of the sacraments and these fears were once common. But the Mass is not first about elements. Communion, not consecration, is the climax. The Mass is some-thing we do. 'Do this in commemoration of me.' At the Mass we are not spectators; we are participants. We are not meant to be

53

passive but active. We are not meant merely to receive, but to receive and give. Offertory is necessary overture. Magic tends to concentrate on elements, but the Mass is an action, a meal which mediates the one, sufficient, sacrifice.

What most sustains and sanctifies every congregation is the way the Mass is presented. Truth cannot be presented without beauty, because truth and beauty are as inseparable as sun and light. The nearest analogy to the action of the Mass is drama. Great drama is truth mediated through beauty, and makes its appeal through aptness of language, structure and presentation. Beauty is not additional to truth; it is the way truth communicates. If a person is true, that person has beauty, for beauty is personal; it is the image of God, not a human artefact.

The Mass badly presented may be constructed as magic. Meaning will be muted, the holy unholied. It may seem so secular, almost desacralized. When do children and teenagers cease going to Mass? Perhaps they cease going to Mass when they no longer believe in magic. But their need for the transcendent, for a more spacious experience of living, still lingers. They still want the transcendent, they still want this contact with a power beyond the finite. They find it in violence, for vandalism gives the confused teenagers a taste of power. It is found in revolution, in political utopias. Or they find it in drugs or in loud, electronic religions.

Catholics may be unaware of the pressures of magic. But the Church is always on its guard. In the last decade the Church abolished the compulsory Friday abstinence. Why? It seemed an excellent practice. The Church abolished compulsory Friday abstinence only because it had lost its meaning. Its meaning was once healthy. It became magic. Good Catholic people would confess to eating meat on a Friday because they thought it was Thursday. That is magic. There is no sin there at all. The priest would explain this to the penitent but would make no impact whatever. What had happened is that the law which is rational had become something else; it had become taboo. And taboo is irrational. Many made tearful confessions, people who had eaten meat by accident and felt they were condemned to eternal torment in consequence. That is magic. And most magic is black magic.

Magic is the religion of the irrational and there is irrationality in us all. Indeed it is the irrational in magic which holds its power to terrify. True religion never frightens; the element which fright-

ens is the magic element. Whole tribes still live in terror of the witch-doctor.

All we seek in this life is a little knowledge, a little power, and an answering love. But the Spirit of love cannot be received directly, because we are not spirits, we are not angels, we are men and women and clothed in weakness. But we need Spirit, and sacraments are agents of that Spirit, divinely-appointed actions, ordained encounters.

The Spirit of God precedes sacrament, and is there from the beginning. The Spirit of God is for man but man can only live through common things like bread and wine and oil and water. These common things can be seen as utilities; matter only, independent of God. They can also be seen as things in their own right but as more; as mediatory of his Spirit.

So the daffodil or the primrose, the lilac, the lilies of the field can be mere subjects for the botanist. Or they can be seen as they were by Christ, as images of the face of the Father. That is the sacramental view of reality. It is that vision which gave us art, gave us the artists, and gave us the poets. But where are they now? Art, poetry, religion go into decline simultaneously, when there is poor vision, when this world is no longer charged with the grandeur of God. The first sacrament is Christ. He is the person, human and divine, who reveals divinity through manhood. 'Through' is the sacramental preposition. Every one of us seeks the ultimate, the absolutely true. Seeks the Father. But there is no access to the Father by direct means, or by the charms of magic. A memorable statement is Christ's simple sentence: 'No one can come to the Father except through me.' That is sacrament – the invisible through the visible; God through the God-man. Blessed are the eyes that see what you see. Blessed, indeed.

55